The Complete Essential Ketogenic Diet Cookbook for Epilepsy

20 Quick and Easy Recipes to manage Epilepsy, Reduce Seizures and Other Disorder Naturally

STEVE K. PARKINS

TABLE OF CONTENTS

INTRODUCTION

DELICIOUS AND EASY TO COOK RECIPES

   1.Avocado and Bacon Omelet

   2.Smoked Salmon and Cream Cheese Roll-Ups

   3.Zucchini Noodles with Pesto Sauce

   4.Grilled Chicken with Lemon Butter Sauce

   5.Cauliflower Crust Pizza

   6.Garlic Butter Shrimp Skewers

   7.Cheesy Cauliflower Rice

   8.Baked Salmon with Dill Sauce

   9.Eggplant Lasagna

   10.Spinach and Feta Stuffed Chicken Breast

   11.Buffalo Chicken Lettuce Wraps

   12.Keto Meatballs in Marinara Sauce

   13.Lemon Garlic Butter Shrimp

   14.Cauliflower Fried Rice

   15.Baked Chicken Thighs with Herbs

   16.Keto Taco Salad

   17.Zucchini Noodles with Pesto

   18.Bacon-Wrapped Asparagus

   19.Keto Chocolate Avocado Pudding

   20.Keto Pizza Casserole

CONCLUSION

INTRODUCTION

In a small town, lived a young girl named Emily who had been battling epilepsy since childhood. Seizures were a constant disruption in her life, causing her immense frustration and limiting her potential. However, hope arrived in an unexpected form – a ketogenic diet cookbook specifically tailored for epilepsy.

Eager to take control of her condition, Emily dove into the cookbook's pages, discovering a wealth of recipes designed to support a ketogenic diet. The ketogenic diet, low in carbohydrates and high in healthy fats, had been known to alleviate seizures in some epilepsy patients.

As Emily embraced the ketogenic lifestyle, she experienced remarkable changes. Her seizures became less frequent and less severe, giving her newfound freedom and a renewed sense of hope. The carefully crafted recipes not only nourished her body but also delighted her taste buds. From delicious avocado and bacon omelets to creamy cauliflower mash and indulgent dark chocolate fat bombs, the cookbook offered a variety of options that made her journey enjoyable and sustainable.

Through her journey, Emily realized the immense benefits of a ketogenic diet for epilepsy. It not only provided her with seizure control but also improved her mental clarity and energy levels. With each passing day, she felt empowered and inspired to live her life to the fullest.

Emily's story is just one of many that highlights the transformative power of a ketogenic diet for epilepsy. The ketogenic diet cookbook serves as a guiding light, providing individuals and their loved ones with the tools they need to navigate this dietary approach and embrace a life free from the shackles of seizures.

Are you or someone you know seeking relief from epilepsy through dietary interventions? Let the ketogenic diet cookbook be your ally on this remarkable journey. Experience the profound benefits of a ketogenic lifestyle and reclaim control over your health. Your story of triumph awaits, and the ketogenic diet cookbook will guide you every step of the way.

DELICIOUS AND EASY TO COOK RECIPES

1.Avocado and Bacon Omelet

Ingredients

3 eggs

2 slices of bacon, cooked and crumbled

1/2 avocado, diced

Salt and pepper to taste

Preparation

Salt and pepper the eggs in a bowl after whisking them.

Heat a non-stick skillet over medium heat and pour in the beaten eggs.

Cook for a few minutes until the omelet starts to set.

Sprinkle the bacon and avocado on one side of the omelet.

Over the filling, fold the other half of the omelet.

Cook for another minute or until the omelet is fully set.

Serve hot.

2.Smoked Salmon and Cream Cheese Roll-Ups

Ingredients

4 slices of smoked salmon

4 tablespoons of cream cheese

1 tablespoon of chopped fresh dill

Juice of half a lemon

Preparation

Lay the smoked salmon slices flat on a clean surface.

Spread a tablespoon of cream cheese on each slice.

Sprinkle chopped dill evenly over the cream cheese.

Squeeze lemon juice over the roll-ups.

Roll up the salmon slices tightly.

Slice into bite-sized pieces.

Serve chilled.

3.Zucchini Noodles with Pesto Sauce

Ingredients

2 medium zucchinis, spiralized into noodles

1/4 cup of fresh basil leaves

2 tablespoons of pine nuts

2 cloves of garlic

1/4 cup of grated Parmesan cheese

3 tablespoons of extra-virgin olive oil

Salt and pepper to taste

Preparation

In a blender or food processor, combine basil leaves, pine nuts, garlic, Parmesan cheese, and olive oil.

If extra olive oil is required, blend the mixture until it is smooth.

Season with salt and pepper to taste.

In a pan, heat a drizzle of olive oil over medium heat.

Add the zucchini noodles and sauté for 2-3 minutes until they soften.

Pour the pesto sauce over the noodles and toss to coat.

Cook for another minute, then remove from heat.

Serve warm.

4.Grilled Chicken with Lemon Butter Sauce

Ingredients

2 boneless, skinless chicken breasts

2 tablespoons of butter, melted

Juice of 1 lemon

2 cloves of garlic, minced

Salt and pepper to taste

Preparation

Preheat a grill or grill pan over medium-high heat.

Season the chicken breasts with salt and pepper.

Grill the chicken for 6-8 minutes per side or until cooked through.

In a small bowl, whisk together melted butter, lemon juice, minced garlic, salt, and pepper.

Remove the chicken from the grill and brush the lemon butter sauce over the chicken breasts.

Let the chicken rest for a few minutes, then slice and serve.

5.Cauliflower Crust Pizza

Ingredients

1 medium cauliflower head, grated

2 eggs

1/2 cup of grated Parmesan cheese

1 teaspoon of dried oregano

1/2 teaspoon of garlic powder

Salt and pepper to taste

Pizza sauce, cheese, and desired toppings

Preparation

Preheat the oven to 425°F (220°C) and line a baking sheet with parchment paper.

Place the grated cauliflower in a microwave-safe bowl and microwave for 5-6 minutes until soft.

Let the cauliflower cool, then transfer it to a clean kitchen towel and squeeze out any excess moisture.

In a bowl, combine the cauliflower, eggs, Parmesan cheese, oregano, garlic powder, salt, and pepper. Mix well.

Transfer the mixture to the prepared baking sheet and shape it into a round pizza crust.

Bake for 15-20 minutes until the crust is golden and crispy.

Remove from the oven and add pizza sauce, cheese, and desired toppings.

Return the pizza to the oven and bake for an additional 10-15 minutes until the cheese is melted and bubbly.

Slice and serve hot.

6.Garlic Butter Shrimp Skewers

Ingredients

1 pound of shrimp, peeled and deveined

3 tablespoons of butter, melted

2 cloves of garlic, minced

Juice of half a lemon

Salt and pepper to taste

Preparation

Preheat a grill or grill pan over medium-high heat.

In a bowl, combine melted butter, minced garlic, lemon juice, salt, and pepper.

Thread the shrimp onto skewers.

Brush the garlic butter mixture over the shrimp.

Grill the shrimp skewers for 2-3 minutes per side until cooked through.

Remove from the grill and serve hot.

7.Cheesy Cauliflower Rice

Ingredients

1 medium cauliflower head, grated or processed into rice-like texture

2 tablespoons of butter

1/2 cup of shredded cheddar cheese

Salt and pepper to taste

Preparation

In a large skillet, melt the butter over medium heat.

Add the cauliflower rice to the skillet and sauté for 5-6 minutes until softened.

Stir in the shredded cheddar cheese until melted and well combined.

Season with salt and pepper to taste.

Remove from heat and serve as a side dish.

8.Baked Salmon with Dill Sauce

Ingredients

2 salmon fillets

2 tablespoons of olive oil

Juice of half a lemon

1 tablespoon of chopped fresh dill

Salt and pepper to taste

Preparation

Preheat the oven to 400°F (200°C) and line a baking sheet with parchment paper.

Place the salmon fillets on the prepared baking sheet.

Drizzle the olive oil and lemon juice over the salmon.

Sprinkle chopped dill, salt, and pepper evenly over the fillets.

Bake for 12-15 minutes until the salmon is cooked through and flakes easily with a fork.

Remove from the oven and serve hot with a dollop of dill sauce.

9.Eggplant Lasagna

Ingredients

1 large eggplant, sliced lengthwise into thin strips

1 pound of ground beef

1 cup of low-carb marinara sauce

1 cup of shredded mozzarella cheese

1/4 cup of grated Parmesan cheese

2 tablespoons of olive oil

Salt and pepper to taste

Preparation

Preheat the oven to 375°F (190°C) and grease a baking dish.

Heat olive oil in a skillet over medium heat.

Add the ground beef and cook until browned. Season with salt and pepper.

Stir in the marinara sauce and simmer for a few minutes.

Layer the eggplant slices in the greased baking dish.

Spread the meat sauce over the eggplant slices.

Sprinkle shredded mozzarella and grated Parmesan cheese over the sauce.

Repeat the layers until all ingredients are used, ending with a layer of cheese on top.

Bake for 25-30 minutes until the cheese is melted and bubbly.

Let it cool slightly before serving.

10.Spinach and Feta Stuffed Chicken Breast

Ingredients

2 boneless, skinless chicken breasts

2 cups of fresh spinach, chopped

1/2 cup of crumbled feta cheese

2 cloves of garlic, minced

2 tablespoons of olive oil

Salt and pepper to taste

Preparation

Preheat the oven to 375°F (190°C) and grease a baking dish.

In a skillet, heat olive oil over medium heat.

Add minced garlic and sauté for a minute until fragrant.

Add chopped spinach and cook until wilted.

Remove from heat and let it cool slightly.

Slice a pocket into each chicken breast, being careful not to cut all the way through.

Stuff each chicken breast with the spinach mixture and crumbled feta cheese.

Chicken breasts should be salted and peppered.

In the baking dish that has been greased, put the stuffed chicken breasts.

Bake the chicken for 25 to 30 minutes, or until done.

Before serving, take it out of the oven and allow it to cool for a while.

11.Buffalo Chicken Lettuce Wraps

Ingredients

2 cups of cooked chicken breast, shredded

1/4 cup of hot sauce

2 tablespoons of mayonnaise

1/4 cup of diced celery

Lettuce leaves, for wrapping

Optional toppings diced tomatoes, sliced green onions, crumbled blue cheese

Preparation

In a bowl, combine shredded chicken, hot sauce, mayonnaise, and diced celery.

All components should be thoroughly combined and coated. Spoon the buffalo chicken mixture onto lettuce leaves.

Add desired toppings, such as diced tomatoes, sliced green onions, and crumbled blue cheese.

Roll up the lettuce leaves to form wraps.

Serve chilled as a refreshing and spicy meal option.

12.Keto Meatballs in Marinara Sauce

Ingredients

1 pound of ground beef

1/4 cup of almond flour

1/4 cup of grated Parmesan cheese

1 egg

2 cloves of garlic, minced

1/4 cup of chopped fresh parsley

Salt and pepper to taste

2 cups of low-carb marinara sauce

Preparation

Bake at 375°F (190°C) for 15 minutes with a baking sheet lined with parchment paper.

Ground beef, almond flour, Parmesan cheese, egg, minced garlic, parsley, salt, and pepper should all be combined in a bowl.

All materials should be completely blended after mixing. Shape the mixture into meatballs of desired size and place them on the prepared baking sheet.

Bake for 20-25 minutes until the meatballs are cooked through.

In a separate saucepan, heat the marinara sauce over medium heat until warmed.

Add the baked meatballs to the marinara sauce and simmer for a few minutes.

Serve the meatballs and marinara sauce over zucchini noodles or cauliflower rice for a complete meal.

13.Lemon Garlic Butter Shrimp

Ingredients

1 pound of shrimp, peeled and deveined

4 tablespoons of butter

4 cloves of garlic, minced

Juice of 1 lemon

Salt and pepper to taste

Chopped fresh parsley for garnish

Preparation

Melt butter in a pan over medium heat.

When aromatic, add the minced garlic and sauté for one minute.

The shrimp should be cooked in the skillet for two to three minutes on each side, or until pink and opaque.

Sprinkle salt and pepper on top of the shrimp after adding the lemon juice.

Stir to evenly distribute the lemon garlic butter sauce on the shrimp.

Remove from heat and top with fresh parsley that has been chopped.

Serve hot as a main dish or as a topping for salads or cauliflower rice.

14.Cauliflower Fried Rice

Ingredients

1 medium cauliflower head, grated or processed into rice-like texture

2 tablespoons of coconut oil

1/2 cup of diced onion

1/2 cup of diced carrots

1/2 cup of diced bell peppers

1/2 cup of peas

2 cloves of garlic, minced

2 tablespoons of tamari or soy sauce

2 eggs, beaten

Salt and pepper to taste

Preparation

Heat coconut oil in a large skillet or wok over medium heat.

Add diced onion, carrots, bell peppers, peas, and minced garlic to the skillet.

Sauté the vegetables for 5-6 minutes until they are tender.

Push the vegetables to one side of the skillet and pour the beaten eggs into the empty space.

Scramble the eggs until cooked, then mix them with the sautéed vegetables.

Add the grated cauliflower to the skillet and stir to combine with the vegetables and eggs.

Pour tamari or soy sauce over the cauliflower mixture and stir well.

Cook for an additional 4-5 minutes until the cauliflower is tender.

Season with salt and pepper to taste.

Remove from heat and serve hot as a low-carb alternative to traditional fried rice.

15.Baked Chicken Thighs with Herbs

Ingredients

4 chicken thighs, bone-in and skin-on

2 tablespoons of olive oil

1 teaspoon of dried thyme

1 teaspoon of dried rosemary

1 teaspoon of dried oregano

Salt and pepper to taste

Preparation

A baking sheet should be lined with parchment paper and the oven should be preheated to 400°F (200°C).

Dried thyme, dried rosemary, dried oregano, salt, and pepper should all be combined in a small bowl.

On the prepared baking sheet, put the chicken thighs.

Chicken thighs should be coated uniformly with olive oil after being drizzled over them.

Making sure the chicken is well-seasoned on all sides, sprinkle the herb mixture over the meat.

Bake the chicken for 25 to 30 minutes, or until the skin is crispy and the meat is thoroughly cooked.

Before serving, take it out of the oven and allow it to cool for a while.

16.Keto Taco Salad

Ingredients

1 pound of ground beef

1 packet of taco seasoning (check for low-carb or homemade options)

1/2 cup of diced tomatoes

1/2 cup of diced onions

1/2 cup of diced bell peppers

1/2 cup of shredded cheddar cheese

1/4 cup of sliced black olives

1/4 cup of sour cream

1/4 cup of guacamole

Lettuce leaves, for serving

Preparation

In a skillet, cook ground beef over medium heat until browned.

Drain excess grease and add the taco seasoning, following the instructions on the packet.

Stir well to coat the ground beef in the seasoning.

In a large bowl, combine diced tomatoes, onions, bell peppers, shredded cheddar cheese, and sliced black olives.

Place lettuce leaves on a plate and spoon the ground beef mixture over the lettuce.

Top with the vegetable and cheese mixture.

Add dollops of sour cream and guacamole on top.

Toss gently to combine all the flavors.

Serve as a satisfying and low-carb taco salad.

17.Zucchini Noodles with Pesto

Ingredients

2 medium zucchini, spiralized into noodles

1/4 cup of homemade or store-bought pesto sauce (check for low-carb options)

1/4 cup of grated Parmesan cheese

Salt and pepper to taste

Preparation

Heat a skillet over medium heat.

Add the zucchini noodles to the skillet and cook for 2-3 minutes until slightly softened.

The pesto sauce should be thoroughly mixed into the pasta.

Cook for 2 more minutes, or until well heated.

After removing from the fire, top the noodles with grated Parmesan cheese.

To taste, add salt and pepper to the food.

Use as a tasty and light substitute for spaghetti.

N.B IF YOU FIND DIFFICULTY IN PREPARING ANY RECIPE YOU CAN CONTACT ME FOR FREE CONSULTATION ON steveparkinshelpcentre@gmail.com

18.Bacon-Wrapped Asparagus

Ingredients

1 bunch of asparagus spears

8-10 slices of bacon

Salt and pepper to taste

Preparation

A baking sheet should be lined with parchment paper and the oven should be preheated to 400°F (200°C).

Trim the woody ends of the asparagus spears.

Divide the asparagus into bundles of 3-4 spears.

Wrap a slice of bacon around each asparagus bundle, starting from the bottom and spiraling up.

Place the bacon-wrapped asparagus bundles on the prepared baking sheet.

Season with salt and pepper.

Bake for 20-25 minutes until the bacon is crispy and the asparagus is tender.

Remove from the oven and let it cool slightly before serving.

19.Keto Chocolate Avocado Pudding

Ingredients

2 ripe avocados, peeled and pitted

1/4 cup of unsweetened cocoa powder

1/4 cup of coconut milk

2 tablespoons of low-carb sweetener (e.g., erythritol or stevia)

1 teaspoon of vanilla extract

Optional toppings whipped cream, chopped nuts, shredded coconut

Preparation

In a blender or food processor, combine avocados, cocoa powder, coconut milk, low-carb sweetener, and vanilla extract.

Blend until smooth and creamy.

Taste and adjust the sweetness if needed.

Transfer the chocolate avocado pudding to serving bowls.

Chill in the refrigerator for at least 1 hour to set.

Before serving, add desired toppings such as whipped cream, chopped nuts, or shredded coconut.

Enjoy as a rich and indulgent dessert option.

20. Keto Pizza Casserole

Ingredients

1 pound of ground beef

1/2 cup of low-carb pizza sauce

1 cup of shredded mozzarella cheese

1/4 cup of sliced pepperoni

1/4 cup of sliced black olives

1/4 cup of diced green bell peppers

1/4 cup of diced onions

1/2 teaspoon of dried oregano

1/2 teaspoon of dried basil

Salt and pepper to taste

Preparation

Preheat the oven to 375°F (190°C) and grease a baking dish.

In a skillet, cook ground beef over medium heat until browned.

Drain excess grease and stir in the low-carb pizza sauce.

Season with dried oregano, dried basil, salt, and pepper.

Spread the ground beef mixture evenly in the prepared baking dish.

Top with shredded mozzarella cheese, sliced pepperoni, sliced black olives, diced bell peppers, and diced onions.

Bake for 20-25 minutes until the cheese is melted and bubbly.

Remove from the oven and let it cool for a few minutes before serving.

CONCLUSION

In conclusion, a ketogenic diet cookbook for epilepsy can be a transformative resource for individuals seeking to manage their condition through dietary interventions. This specialized cookbook offers a wide range of recipes that adhere to the principles of a ketogenic diet, which is known to have significant benefits for epilepsy patients.

By following the recipes in this cookbook, individuals can embrace a diet that is low in carbohydrates and high in healthy fats, effectively inducing a state of ketosis in the body. Ketosis has been shown to reduce seizure activity and provide relief for those living with epilepsy.

The cookbook not only provides delicious and nutritious recipes but also empowers individuals to take control of their health and make positive dietary choices. Each recipe is carefully crafted to ensure a proper balance of macronutrients, essential vitamins, and minerals that support overall well-being.

Moreover, the cookbook serves as a valuable educational tool, offering insights into the science behind the ketogenic diet and its effects on epilepsy. It provides practical guidance on meal planning, grocery shopping, and cooking techniques specific to the diet.

By embracing the ketogenic diet with the help of this cookbook, individuals can experience improved seizure control, increased energy levels, mental clarity, and overall better health. It is a powerful resource that can unlock a world of culinary possibilities while positively impacting the lives of those living with epilepsy.

Take the first step towards a healthier and seizure-free life by investing in this ketogenic diet cookbook for epilepsy. Empower yourself with knowledge, embrace the transformative power of food, and embark on a journey to better health and well-being.

HAPPY READING

N.B IF YOU FIND DIFFICULTY PREPARING ANY RECIPE YOU CAN CONTACT ME FOR FREE CONSULTATION ON steveparkinshelpcentre@gmail.com

Made in the USA
Columbia, SC
18 December 2024

49771969R00017